How We Use

Coal

Chris Oxlade

Raintree

Chicago, Illinois

For more information address the publisher:
Raintree, 100 N. LaSalle, Suite 1200, Chicago IL 60602

Printed and bound in China by South China
  Printing Company

08 07 06 05 04
10 9 8 7 6 5 4 3 2 1

Library of Congress Cataloging-in-Publication Data:
Oxlade, Chris.
  How we use coal / Chris Oxlade.
     p. cm. -- (Using materials)
Includes bibliographical references and index.
Contents: Coal and its properties -- Where coal comes
from -- Mining coal -- Types of coal -- Coal for heat --
Smokeless coal -- Coal for power -- Coal for moving --
Coal and coke -- More fuels from coal -- Coal tar -- Peat
-- Coal and the environment.
  ISBN 1-4109-0592-6 (hc) 1-4109-0991-3 (pb)
  1. Coal--Juvenile literature. [1. Coal.] I. Title. II.
Series:
Oxlade, Chris. Using materials.
  TN801.O95 2004
  662.6'2--dc21
                              2003007

Acknowledgments
The publishers would like to thank the following for
permission to reproduce photographs:
p.4 Larry Lee Photography/Corbis, p. 5 Hiene
Scheebeli/Photo Researchers Inc.; pp .6, 10 Steve
McCutcheon/Visuals Unlimited; p. 7 Hulton-Deutsch
Collection/Corbis; pp. 8, 24 Gayle Mault/Ace Library;
p.9 H. David Seawell/Corbis; pp. 11, 25 Science VU;
p.12 Andy Butler/Eye Ubiquitous/Corbis; p. 13John T.
Fowler; p. 14 Inga Spence; p. 15 John D. Cunningham;
p. 16 David Wasserman/Brand X Pictures; p. 17
Cordelia Molloy/Science Photo Library; p. 18 George
H. Huey/ Corbis; p. 19 James A. Sugar/Corbis; p. 20
AFP/Corbis; p. 21 Dennis Gottlieb/Foodpix; p. 22 Mike
French/Meonshore Studios Limited; p.23 Peter and
Georgina Bowaterp; p. 26 Michael St. Maur
Sheil/Corbis; p. 27 Lee Snider/Image Works; p. 28
Lester Lefkowitz/Corbis; p. 29 Will and Deni
McIntyre/Corbis.

Cover photographs reproduced with permission of
Corbis (top) and Photo Researchers Inc. (C. Molloy)
(bottom).

Every effort has been made to contact copyright
holders of any material reproduced in this book. Any
omissions will be rectified in subsequent printings if
notice is given to the publishers.

Contents

Any words appearing in bold, **like this,** are explained in the Glossary.

Coal and Its Properties

All the objects we use from day to day are made from materials. Coal is a material. Most coal is used as **fuel** because it burns well. **Coal tar** is one of the materials we get from coal. We use coal tar in some medicines because it can be good for skin problems. It is also used for making roofs because it is **waterproof.**

Coal is a type of rock. We get it from the ground.

We burn more coal for heating and making **electricity** than any other fuel.

Properties tell us what a material is like. Coal is a **solid,** and is black or dark brown. Coal is brittle. This means it breaks apart easily and crumbles into dust. We get other materials from coal by splitting it up into different parts.

Don't use it!

The different properties of materials make them useful for different jobs. For example, we would not use coal to make containers. They would break easily and make the things inside dirty.

Where Does Coal Come From?

Coal is a **natural** material. The coal we use today was made millions of years ago. When bushes, tropical trees, and other plants died and fell into **swamps,** they were gradually buried by mud and rocks. Over millions of years the dead plants turned into coal. Some coal is made from plants that lived before the dinosaurs. We call coal a **fossil fuel.**

This seam of black coal in Arkansas is trapped by layers of other rocks.

One hundred years ago steam ships ran on coal. Workers shoveled coal into fires to keep the engines running.

Coal in history

*Coal was burned as a **fuel** in China more than 3,000 years ago. It became a much more important material about 250 years ago. Then coal started to be used as a fuel in steam engines, and for making large quantities of iron.*

We find coal in layers in the ground called **seams.** There are other layers of rocks above and below the coal. Scientists called geologists try to figure out where there might be coal seams hidden underground. They drill holes into the ground to see if they are right.

Mining Coal

Getting coal from the ground is called coal **mining.** Sometimes we find coal **seams** on the surface or only a little way underground. We get this coal by surface mining. Miners break up the coal with drills and explosives and scoop up the lumps of coal with diggers. When a coal seam is deep underground, miners have to dig a hole called a shaft. They use drills and huge buckets to lift the coal to the surface.

This machine digs deep underground. It breaks coal from a coal seam.

Coal is broken into small lumps and washed after it is mined.

We find coal in the ground all over the world, but we cannot use all of it. Sometimes coal seams are not big enough to be worth digging up. Sometimes they are too far down to reach.

Danger in the mines

*Going deep underground to dig out coal can be dangerous. There are often **gases** in mines that can explode. Rock can fall on top of miners, and water can flood into mines.*

Types of Coal

There are three types of coal. The **properties** of each type are slightly different. Each one also contains a different amount of a substance called **carbon.** Carbon is the part of coal that burns.

Anthracite is a type of coal that is nearly all carbon. Anthracite is hard, black, and shiny. It is difficult to set on fire, but it burns very well. It makes a lot of heat and hardly any smoke or odor.

Anthracite is black and shiny.

Bituminous coal is the most common form of coal used today.

Almost all the coal we use is called **bituminous** coal. It contains slightly less carbon than anthracite but it burns well and makes only a little smoke.

The third type of coal is called **lignite.** Only about half of lignite is carbon. Lignite is brown and crumbly. It makes much less heat than anthracite or bituminous coal, and is very smoky. Lignite is burned mostly in homes and power plants.

Coal for Heat

The most important property of coal is that it burns well. When it burns it gives off a lot of heat. This is why we use coal as a **fuel.** About three-quarters of all the coal that is **mined** from the ground is burned as fuel. Most of this coal is burned in power plants to make **electricity.** Lumps of coal burn slowly, so they keep giving off heat for a long time.

Only the outside of coal burns.

After coal has burned, gray dust called ash is left over. We have to get rid of the ash before we burn more coal.

In some countries coal is also a fuel for cooking and heating in homes, offices, and factories. The best type of coal for heating and cooking is **anthracite.** It can be used on open fires, in stoves, or in central-heating boilers.

Don't use it!
*In some places coal is not used for heating homes as much as it was many years ago. It has been replaced with cleaner fuels such as **natural gas.***

Coal for Power

Almost all coal that is dug up is burned in power plants to make **electricity** for homes, schools, offices, and factories. Most power plants burn **bituminous** coal because there is plenty of it. It also burns faster than **anthracite** and gives out lots of heat. **Lignite** gives out much less heat than bituminous coal. It is only used in power plants that are very close to lignite mines.

A power plant burns hundreds of tons of coal every day. The coal is brought by train.

Thick cables carry electricity from the power station to nearby towns and cities.

Coal to electricity

Inside a power plant the coal is crushed to make powder. Powder burns much faster than big lumps of coal. The heat from the burning powdered coal boils water to make steam. The steam rushes through huge fans called **turbines,** making them spin around very fast. The turbines turn machines called generators that make electricity.

Smokeless Coal

When coal burns it makes smoke that rises into the air. The smoke looks gray because it contains tiny bits of **carbon** that did not burn properly. If there are a lot of coal fires close together the smoke can cause thick fog called **smog.** Smog is dangerous for people who have asthma and other breathing problems.

Tiny pieces of unburned coal and ash are carried upward by the hot rising **gases** from the fire.

Coal that burns with very little smoke is better for the environment.

To stop smog from happening, many towns and cities around the world have banned people from burning coal that makes smoke. Instead, people must burn smokeless coal. **Bituminous** coal is made smokeless by heating it up but not letting it burn. This gets rid of the substances in the coal that cause smoke. **Anthracite** produces only a little smoke.

Coal for Moving

One hundred years ago nearly all trains and ships had steam engines. The steam engines worked using heat from coal. Coal was burned on a fire underneath a tank of water called a boiler. The heat from the coal boiled the water to make steam and the steam pushed and pulled on **pistons.** In a steam train the pistons turned the wheels. In a ship the pistons turned the propeller.

This is a steam train. Steam from the boiler pushes and pulls the piston to make the wheels turn.

This man is shoveling coal into the furnace of a steam train.

There are still some steam trains around the world. Most trains run on diesel engines or **electricity.** The power for electric trains can still come from burning coal, but in a power plant many miles away. Most modern ships have diesel engines or use oil instead of coal to heat their boilers.

Don't use it!

Coal burns well, but slowly. So we cannot use coal for some jobs. For example, we could not use coal instead of gasoline in a car engine. It would burn too slowly and clog up the engine.

Coal and Coke

We do not burn all the coal that is **mined.** Coal is made up of many useful substances. These substances are lost when coal is burned. We get the substances from the coal by heating it in a very hot oven where there is no air. Because there is no air the coal doesn't burn. A lot of hot **gases** come out of the coal instead.

This melted iron was made using coke.

Barbecue fuel is also made from coke.

A dark, gray **solid** material is left behind in the oven. It is called coke. Coke is lighter than coal and has small holes in it. Almost all the coke made is used as a **raw material** for making iron and steel. The coke is burned in a furnace with iron **ore.** The **carbon** in the coke helps to separate the iron from the ore.

Coal Tar

The **gases** from a coke-making oven do not go to waste. When they cool down they turn into useful materials. **Coal tar** is a black, oily **liquid** made when **bituminous** coal is turned into coke. Coal-tar soap and ointments for itchy skin contain substances from coal tar. Some **fertilizers** that help plants to grow also contain coal tar.

Coal-tar soap can be good for some skin problems.

This black liquid is called creosote. It comes from coal tar. It helps to keep wood from **rotting.**

Pitch

Pitch is a black, sticky, **waterproof solid** that comes from coal tar. Builders put pitch on roofs to stop water from leaking through. Pitch is also used to make road surfaces. It makes the small bits of rock in the road surface stick together and stops water from getting into the road.

Don't use it!

Coal tar helps to soothe some itchy skin problems. Many skin ointments contain just a little coal tar. We would not put only coal tar straight onto our skin, because it might cause a rash.

More Fuels From Coal

Another **gas** that comes from a coke-making oven is called coal gas. Coal gas burns very well. It is used as a **fuel** to heat the coke-making ovens. Fifty years ago coal gas was supplied to people's houses. It burned in gas stoves for cooking and in gas lamps that lit homes.

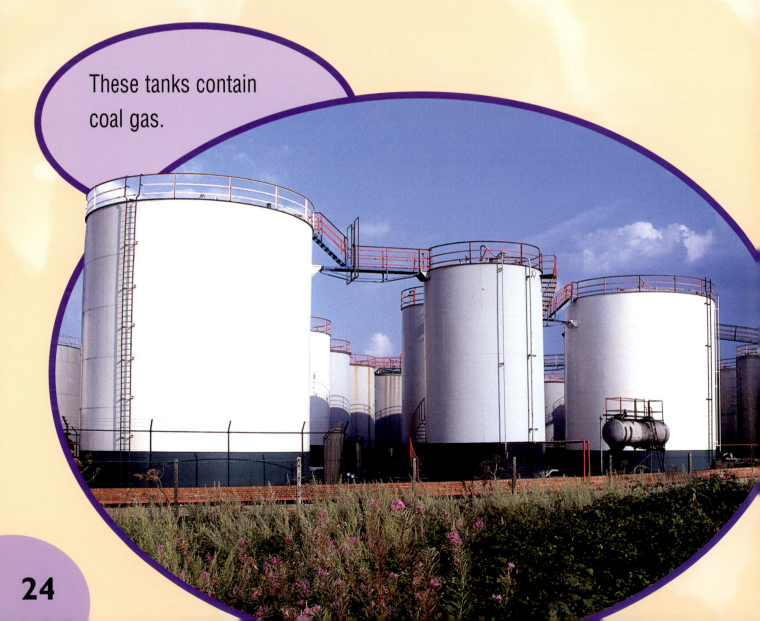

These tanks contain coal gas.

This is natural gas burning on a stove. Natural gas replaced coal gas about 50 years ago.

Changing coal

We can change **solid** coal into gases or **liquids** to burn as fuels. Turning coal into gas is called gasification. Turning coal into liquid is called liquefaction. This makes coal into gasoline for engines and fuel oil for heating. Right now we do not use these ways because we get fuels from crude oil and **natural** gas. We may have to use them eventually, however, because supplies of crude oil and natural gas will run out.

Don't use it!
Coal gas burns well but it makes black dust called soot. We now use natural gas instead of coal gas for cooking because natural gas does not make soot.

Peat

When plants that live in bogs or **swamps** die their remains fall into the water. They do not completely **rot** away in the water. They are gradually buried under more remains. Over hundreds of years a layer of spongy material builds up. This material is called peat. If peat gets buried under layers of rock it slowly turns to coal.

These workers are digging peat from a peat bog.

Some peat is squashed into small blocks called peat briquettes.

When peat is dried it burns very well. It is an important **fuel** in some parts of the world, such as Ireland. The peat is dug from a peat bog. It is very wet so it must be dried before it can be burned. Peat is also used as a **fertilizer** because it contains lots of minerals for the soil.

Don't use it!

Peat comes from places called peat bogs. They are important **habitats** *for many plants and animals. Some people think that we should not dig up peat for garden fertilizer. They say we are destroying habitats just to make our plants grow better.*

Coal and the Environment

When coal burns it gives off smoke. Smoke contains tiny bits of unburned coal that causes **smog** and makes people sick. We can reduce smoke by using smokeless **fuels.** In many power plants the particles are trapped before they can get into the air. This helps to keep the air clean.

We still burn smoky coal in many places. The smoke can travel hundreds of miles in the air.

28

These trees were killed by acid rain.

Burning coal also gives off **gases** that are changing the earth's atmosphere. One of the gases is carbon dioxide. This is one of the gases causing global warming, which is making our weather change. Coal also contains a lot of a substance called sulfur. When the sulfur gets into the air it turns rain into an **acid.** Acid rain harms trees and wildlife.

Mining

Getting coal from the ground also spoils the environment. **Mines** make the countryside look ugly and destroy the homes of the wildlife that lives there. Harmful substances are made when coal is cleaned before it is burned. These can get into rivers and poison wildlife as well.

Find Out for Yourself

The best way to find out more about coal is to investigate for yourself. If you live close to a power plant or factory, look out for smoke coming from chimneys. How do you think the coal is used? You will find the answers to many of your questions in this book. You can also look in other books and on the Internet.

Books to read

Ballard, Carol. *Science Answers: Grouping Materials: From Gold to Wool*. Chicago: Heinemann Library, 2003.

Hunter, Rebecca. *Discovering Science: Matter*. Chicago: Raintree, 2001.

Using the Internet

Try searching the Internet to find out about things having to do with coal. Websites can change, so if one of the links below no longer works, don't worry. Use a search engine, such as www.Yahooligans.com or www.internet4kids.com. For example, you could try searching using the keywords "smokeless coal," "steam train," and "acid rain."

Websites

www.bbc.co.uk/schools/revisewise/science/materials/
A great site that explains all about different materials.

www.enviroliteracy.org/subcategory.php/21.html
Learn more about the use of coal and other fossil fuels from the Environmental Literacy Council.

Glossary

acid liquid that eats away at materials

anthracite hard type of coal that contains a lot of carbon

bituminous type of coal

carbon part of coal that burns

coal tar black, oily liquid that comes from coal

electricity kind of energy that flows along wires. Much of the electricity we use at home is made at power plants using heat from burning coal.

fertilizer material that contains minerals that plants use to grow better

fossil fuel fuel made from the remains of animals and plants that died millions of years ago. Coal, oil, and natural gas are fossil fuels.

fuel material that burns well, making plenty of heat

gas substance, like air, that spreads out to fill the space it is in

habitat place where an animal or a plant lives. For example, a forest is a habitat.

lignite soft type of coal

liquid wet substance, like water, that you can pour

mine place where coal or another material is dug from the ground

natural describes anything that is not made by people

ore rock from which certain types of metal can be taken

piston part of an engine that is moved by steam or burning gas

property quality of a material that tells us what it is like. Hard, soft, bendable, and strong are all properties.

raw material material that is used to make other materials

rot to be broken down into simpler substances

seam layer of coal under the ground

smog thick fog caused by smoke in the atmosphere

solid substance that is hard, something that is not a liquid or a gas

swamp ground covered in shallow water

turbine machine like a propeller that turns when steam flows through it

waterproof describes a material that does not let water flow through it

Index